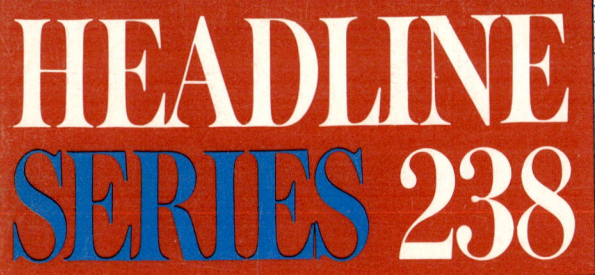

HEADLINE SERIES 238

FOREIGN POLICY ASSOCIATION

DISCARD

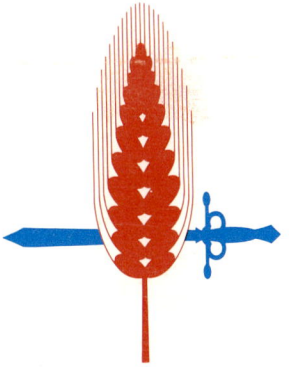

Human Needs AND THE Security of Nations

by
LESTER R. BROWN

Human Needs and the Security of Nations

by Lester R. Russell Brown

CONTENTS

1. What Is National Security? 3
2. Population 8
3. The Lagging Energy Transition 16
4. Deteriorating mainly Biological Systems 24
5. Climate Modification 33
6. Global Food Insecurity 38
7. Economic Threats to Security 46
8. Security and Human Needs 55

Talking It Over 61

HEADLINE Series 238, February 1978 $1.40

Cover design: Samuel N. Antupit

The Author

LESTER R. BROWN is president of the Worldwatch Institute in Washington, D.C. For ten years ending in 1969 he served in the U.S. Department of Agriculture, where for three years he administered the International Agricultural Development Service. His writings on food, population and international affairs include *Man, Land and Food* (1963), *Seeds of Change* (1970), *World Without Borders* (1972), *In the Human Interest: A Strategy to Stabilize World Population* (1974) and, in the same year, *By Bread Alone*, an adaptation of which was published as HEADLINE Series 225 under the title, "Our Daily Bread."

The Foreign Policy Association

The Foreign Policy Association is a private, nonprofit, nonpartisan educational organization. Its purpose is to stimulate wider interest and more effective participation in, and greater understanding of, world affairs among American citizens. Among its activities is the continuous publication, dating from 1935, of the HEADLINE Series pamphlets. The authors of these pamphlets are responsible for factual accuracy and for the views expressed. FPA itself takes no position on issues of United States foreign policy.

Editorial Advisory Committee:
Carol Edler Baumann
W. Phillips Davison
Keith Goldhammer
Antonie T. Knoppers

Hans J. Morgenthau, *chairman.*
William H. McNeill
Edwin Newman
Joan E. Spero
Richard H. Ullman

HEADLINE Series, No. 238, February 1978, published February, April, June, October and December by the Foreign Policy Association, Inc., 345 E. 46th St., New York, N.Y. 10017. Chairman, Carter L. Burgess; Editor, Wallace Irwin, Jr.; Associate Editor, Gwen Crowe. Subscription rates, $7.00 for 5 issues; $13.00 for 10 issues; $18.00 for 15 issues. Single copies, $1.40. Second-class postage paid at New York, N.Y. Copyright 1978 by Foreign Policy Association, Inc. Composed and printed at Science Press, Ephrata, Penn.

Library of Congress Catalog No. 78-51516

1

What Is National Security?

The term "national security" has become a commonplace expression, a concept regularly appealed to. It is used to justify the maintenance of armies, the development of new weapons systems, and the manufacture of armaments. A fourth of all the Federal taxes in the United States and at least an equivalent amount in the Soviet Union are levied in its name.

The concern for the security of a nation is undoubtedly as old as the nation state itself, but since World War II the concept of national security has acquired an overwhelmingly military character. Commonly veiled in secrecy, considerations of military threats have become so dominant that other threats to the security of nations have often been ignored. Accumulating evidence indicates that new threats are emerging, threats with which military forces cannot cope.

This pamphlet is the first of six issues in the HEADLINE *Series, dealing with international topics of special humanistic significance, whose publication over the years 1978-80 is supported by the National Endowment for the Humanities. The present issue is adapted from portions of the author's forthcoming book* The Twenty-Ninth Day, *to be published by W. W. Norton, Inc., New York, in March 1978.*

U.S. Army photograph

Arms may offer security from military attack . . .

The Dominant Military View

The notion that countries everywhere should be prepared to defend themselves at all times from any conceivable external threat is a relatively modern one. As recently as 1939, for example, the United States had a defense budget of only $1.3 billion. Prior to World War II, countries mobilized troops in times of war instead of relying on a large permanent military establishment.

The policy of continual preparedness has led to the militarization of the world economy, with military expenditures now accounting for 6 percent of the global product. Worldwide, the military claims of national budgets exceed health-service appropriations. Most countries spend more on national security than they do on educating their youth. The development of new, "more effective" weapons systems now engages fully a quarter of the world's scientific talent.

World military expenditures in 1976 reached an estimated $350 billion, a sum that exceeds the income of the poorest one-

Wide World Photos

... but security from hunger requires other measures.

half of humanity. At the current rate of weapons procurement, two days of world expenditures on arms equal the annual budget of the United Nations and its specialized agencies. Thirty million men and women in their prime productive years are under arms today.

This competition between the military and social sectors of the world economy is graphically analyzed by Ruth Leger Sivard in *World Military and Social Expenditures 1977*. No attempt will be made to further that analysis here. Nor will any effort be made to assess anew the traditional military threats to national security. Rather, the purpose of this paper is to identify and briefly describe several major new threats to national security, many of which are outside the purview of national security as traditionally defined.

Man and Nature: a New Focus

The overwhelmingly military approach to national security is based on the assumption that the principal threat to security comes from other nations. But the threats to security may now arise less from the relationship of nation to nation and more from the relationship of man to nature. Dwindling reserves of oil and the deterioration of the earth's biological systems now threaten the security of nations everywhere.

National security cannot be maintained unless national economies can be sustained, but, unfortunately, the health of many economies cannot be sustained for much longer without major adjustments. All advanced industrial economies are fueled primarily by oil, a resource that is being depleted. While military strategists have worried about the access of industrial economies to Middle Eastern oil, another more serious threat, the eventual exhaustion of the world's oil supplies, has been moving to the fore. If massive alternative sources of energy are not in place when the projected downturn in world oil production comes some 15 years hence, crippling economic disruptions will result.

While the oil supply is threatened by depletion, the productivity of the earth's principal biological systems—fisheries, forests, grasslands and croplands—is threatened by excessive human claims. These biological systems provide all food and all the raw materials for industry except minerals and petrochemicals. In fishery after fishery, the catch now exceeds the long-term sustainable yield. The cutting of trees exceeds the regenerative capacity of forests almost everywhere. Grasslands are deteriorating on every continent as livestock populations increase along with human population. Croplands, too, are being damaged by erosion as population pressures mount. Failure to arrest this deterioration of biological systems threatens not only the security of individual nations but the survival of civilization as we know it.

The deterioration of the earth's biological systems is not a peripheral issue of concern only to environmentalists. The global economy depends on these biological systems. Anything that threatens their viability threatens the global economy. Any deterioration in these systems represents a deterioration in the human prospect.

Wide World Photos

Food shortages contributed to the fall of Ethiopia's Haile Selassie and threatened regimes of Gierek in Poland and Sadat in Egypt.

As the 70's progress these new threats are becoming more visible. During the decade, food shortages have led to temporary rises in death rates in at least a dozen countries. Indeed, the lives lost to the increase in hunger may exceed the combat casualties in all the international conflicts of the past two decades.

Global food insecurity and the associated instability in food prices have become a common source of political instability. The centuries-old dynasty in Ethiopia came to an end in 1974 not because a foreign power invaded and prevailed but because ecological deterioration precipitated a food crisis and famine. In the summer of 1976 the Polish government was badly shaken by riots when it sought to raise food prices closer to the world level. In 1977, the riots that followed official attempts to raise food prices in Egypt came closer to toppling the government of President Anwar el-Sadat than has Israeli military power.

The need for countries to confront these threats and to address them cooperatively suggests that the military's role in securing a nation's well-being and survival is relatively less important than it once was. At the same time, protecting and securing the future of a nation by strengthening international cooperation, developing alternative energy sources, and producing adequate food supplies are escalating in importance.

2

Population

Human-like creatures have existed for some 60,000 generations, but only during the last generation have human numbers in entire regions of the world grown by 2 to 3 percent per year. Growth rates of this order have come into effect so recently that their impact has not yet been adequately assessed. It is already clear, however, that rapid population growth intensifies almost every important problem with which humanity wrestles.

Before agriculture developed, population growth was imperceptibly slow. The pre-agricultural era, characterized by both high death rates and high birthrates, was a precarious period in human existence. The 12,000 years between the birth of agriculture and the advent of the industrial revolution were marked by gradually accelerating population growth. Beginning only two centuries ago, the industrial revolution further accelerated this growth as advances in industrial technology supported the evolution and expansion of agriculture. By the outbreak of World War II, the annual population increase had reached 1 percent. Thereupon, the burst of scientific innovation and economic activity that began during the 1940's substantially enhanced the earth's food-producing capacity and led to dramatic improvements in disease control. The resulting marked reduction in death rates created an unprecedented imbalance between births and deaths and an explosive rate of world population growth.

How Human Population Growth Accelerated

	Year reached	Interval in years
First billion	1830	2,000,000
Second billion	1930	100
Third billion	1960	30
Fourth billion	1975	15
Fifth billion (projection)	1986	11
Sixth billion (projection)	1995	9

Source: United Nations

Most population growth today occurs in pre-industrial societies. Two countries, China and India, are now contributing 9 million and 12 million respectively to the world's annual increase of 64 million. With a much smaller population base, Mexico adds more people each year than the United States does, and Brazil adds more than the Soviet Union.

The world's population today is young. In many poor countries, more than 40 percent of all people are under 15 years of age; in Nigeria and Peru the figure is 45 percent, and in Pakistan 46 percent. In societies with such age structures, the proportion

In the U.S., Ethiopia, India and Japan, more people crowd the world.

United Nations

United Nations

UN-financed family planning in Indonesia (above) and Bangladesh (right) is helping slow a population surge that, if unchecked, would

of dependent children to economically active adults is high. Moreover, the number of entrants into the job markets in these countries will soon soar.

Although the food dimension of the population threat remains paramount, population growth also contributes to ecological, economic and social stresses. It fans inflation by creating resource scarcities. It raises unemployment by increasing the number of job-seekers faster than jobs are created. Where it outstrips economic growth, it pushes down living standards. It undermines efforts to spread literacy, to improve health services, and to provide housing.

Always a drain on food and other resources, population growth in some situations acts as a double-edged sword, simultaneously increasing demands and reducing supplies. This double-edged effect can readily be seen in fisheries, forests and agriculture. For example, as long as the demand for firewood, wood pulp and lumber is lower than the sustainable yield of the

United Nations

have approximately doubled the population of both countries in the quarter century 1975-2000.

forest, population growth has no impact on production; but once the demand exceeds the sustainable yield, it begins to eat away the productive resource base itself. In economic terms it consumes the principal as well as the interest. Similarly, where population growth leads to urban encroachment on Canadian cropland or to village encroachment on Indian cropland, the effect is the same—reduced food output.

Recent Population Trends

Sometime in the late 1960's, the *rate* of world population growth reached an all-time high and then began to subside. In 1970, human numbers grew by an estimated 1.90 percent. The most recent data show a marked deceleration to 1.64 percent growth in 1975. More than anything else, this progress reflects the widening availability of family planning services—including both contraception and abortion—and the growing desire to use them.

The global slowing of population growth during the 1970's has been concentrated in three geographic regions: Western Europe, North America and East Asia. No achievement is more impressive than the dramatic reduction of population growth in East Asia. If the statistics available to me are accurate, I estimate that the region's growth rate declined from 1.85 percent in 1970 to 1.18 percent in 1975. The estimated reduction in the Chinese crude birthrate from 32 per thousand of total population to 19 per thousand is the most rapid ever recorded for a five-year span.

By contrast, only a few Latin American countries have reduced fertility rates. Among the smaller countries, Costa Rica and Panama have brought down birthrates most effectively. The two largest nations of the region are both late comers to family planning: Mexico's program is barely beginning to show results, while Brazil only indirectly abandoned its pronatalist policy in 1974 when it announced "that family planning should be available to all couples who want it, as a human right, not as a part of a policy to reduce rates of growth."

As of 1976, only six countries, all of them in Europe—East Germany, West Germany, Luxembourg, Austria, Belgium and the United Kingdom—had stable or declining populations. None of these countries has an explicit policy of stabilizing population. But all six enjoy high levels of income, support high levels of education and employment for women, and provide easy access to contraceptives.

Several other countries have birthrates that are now dropping below 15 per thousand and are approaching a balance with death rates. European countries in this group include France, Italy, Sweden, Norway, Denmark, the Netherlands and Switzerland. Also in this group are the United States, the world's fourth most populous country, and Japan, the seventh.

The weightiest demographic unknown among industrial countries concerns Eastern Europe and the Soviet Union, where strong pronatalist policies have prevailed in recent years. Almost all the East European countries face food problems resembling those that led to the 1976 troubles in Poland. Glaring housing shortages in Czechoslovakia can only be aggravated by pronatalist policies. At some point, policy-makers must reconcile such policies with pressing needs. For example, Soviet planners may begin to link population policies to their country's massive and uncomfortable dependence on food imports after poor harvests.

Death from Hunger Reappears

In many poorer countries, the 70's have witnessed sporadic rises in death rates. Neither war nor epidemics but hunger and nutritional stress are to blame. World grain reserves were quickly depleted between 1972 and 1974, and food prices climbed accordingly. Whenever food scarcities develop, the weaker members of society, usually infants and the elderly among the lower income groups, suffer most, since they are least able to withstand the acute physiological stress of near-starvation.

According to the Ford Foundation, in Bangladesh's 1971 war for independence the loss of life in combat was rather small compared with the number of lives claimed by hunger, especially among the very young and the very old. The death rate in Matlab Bazar, a typical rural district, climbed from an average of 15.7 per thousand for 1966-70 to 21.3 in 1971-72. If, as the Ford report suggests, Matlab Bazar is representative of Bangladesh as a whole, then there was a nationwide increase in deaths in that year of some 400,000. Again in 1974-75, when the harvests fell again, the death rate in Matlab Bazar climbed to 20.0 per thousand, suggesting a nationwide excess of deaths of 330,000. On the same basis, the excess of deaths for 1975-76 was calculated at 192,000.

A similar pattern appears in neighboring India. India's poor 1972 harvest came in after food-production efforts slackened following the introduction of the high-yielding dwarf wheats in the late 1960's. When the monsoon failed in the summer of 1972, India had used up its food reserves to aid Bangladesh, while the Soviet Union had secretly tied up most of the world's exportable wheat supplies, leaving little for India or anyone else. Unable to import all the food it needed, the Indian government stood by helplessly while food consumption dropped sharply. The poorer states, heavily dependent on rain-fed crops of sorghum, millet and wheat, were the most severely affected. In the states of Bihar, Orissa and Uttar Pradesh, deaths in 1972 exceeded those of the preceding year by an estimated 830,000.

Outside Asia, the sheer numbers of people caught in the often fatal food squeeze of recent years were fewer, but the plight of the hunger-stricken groups was, if anything, worse. This has been especially true in the African region bordering the Sahara, known as the Sahel, where population pressure on the fragile desert ecosystem has been steadily gathering force. On the southern fringe of the Sahelian zone, a drought beginning in the late 1960's and continuing into the 70's brought the deterioration of land and food supplies into painfully sharp focus. The six countries most seriously affected—Senegal, Mauritania, Niger, Upper Volta, Chad and Mali—together contained 22 million people, many of them nomadic herdsmen wholly dependent on their cattle, goats and camels. As the drought intensified, the nomads sought to sell what emaciated animals remained, but for countless thousands the loss of livestock was total. The once-proud nomads had become "ecological refugees," herded into emergency feeding camps. Thousands made it to the camps so weakened that they died before they could be revived. Many perished en route. After a tour of the Sahelian zone, Professor Michael Latham, a Cornell nutritionist, testified before a congressional committee that the number of lives lost was probably somewhere between 100,000 and a quarter of a million.

Farther east in Africa, the ecological deterioration of Ethiopia's food system was also brought into focus by a drought. This situation eventually claimed 200,000 lives and brought the 47-year reign of Emperor Haile Selassie to an end. In Somalia, too, thousands died of severe malnutrition and disease, and many of the victims perished after they reached relief camps.

Population Stabilization: a New Urgency

UN projections show world population increasing from the current 4 billion to some 10 billion to 16 billion before eventually leveling off. From a purely demographic point of view, these projections are quite sound. But when viewed in the larger picture of ecological stresses, technologies and social structures, they do not hold up. Signs of stress on the world's principal biological systems—forests, fisheries, grasslands and croplands—indicate that in many places these systems have already reached the breaking point. Expecting them to withstand a tripling or quadrupling of population pressures defies ecological reality.

Already, the goal of national population policies has shifted in several countries during the 1970's from slowing population growth to stabilizing population. Among these countries are the world's two most populous, China and India, as well as Mexico and Bangladesh. India, in fact, found itself in 1976 publicly considering the use, as a last resort, of compulsory sterilization of parents with three or more children.

In the years ahead, however, governments in other countries may also consider drastic action out of desperation. At least a score of countries, such as Algeria and Mexico, already have experienced a quarter century of annual population growth at 3 percent or more. If they delay too long, such countries will be forced to cope with mass migration into neighboring countries, strong incentives to limit family size, or loss of life on a scale experienced during the 1970's by Bangladesh, India and Ethiopia.

3
The Lagging Energy Transition

When the Arab oil embargo was imposed in late 1973, it underlined the vulnerability of oil-importing countries everywhere. Since then attention has focused on the threats to national security posed by such disruptions. President Gerald R. Ford and Secretary of State Henry A. Kissinger hinted strongly at a military invasion of the Middle Eastern oil fields in the event of another threat to the oil "lifeline" to the Western industrial countries.

In their preoccupation with short-term supply disruptions, strategic planners have lost sight of a far more central fact: namely, that oil reserves are being rapidly depleted and that the downturn in world oil production may be only a decade and a half away. It is the failure to prepare for this eventuality that poses the real threat to the future security of oil-dependent nations.

The Arab oil embargo of late 1973, temporary though it was, did provide some clues as to what a world with shrinking oil supplies would be like. Early in 1974, American motorists found themselves sitting in long lines at service stations. Some waited with anger and frustration, others with resignation for their turn at the gasoline pump. Half a world away wheat farmers in North India sat in line on the ground at the local petrol station with five-gallon fuel cans waiting for a delivery of gasoline for

Vivid memory: long gasoline queues in New York, December 1973

their irrigation pumps. Many held their place in the queue for days but the gasoline never came. The shortage of irrigation fuel reduced the wheat harvest by a million tons, enough to feed 6 million Indians for one year. For American motorists and Punjabi wheat farmers, the energy crisis was at least temporarily a reality.

The harsh winter weather of early 1977 found the United States short of natural gas, a principal fuel used for both household and industrial purposes. An uncommonly severe winter, coupled with the lack of an effective conservation program, had led to critical shortages in several northeastern and midwestern states. As factories were forced to close, an estimated 1.8 million workers were laid off, adding to already widespread unemployment. Schools were closed and stores curbed their business hours.

An Approaching Crisis

These graphic shortages in the United States and India should not be viewed as rare or random events. Rather they should be seen as advance warnings of an unfolding crisis of vast proportions, one that is almost certain to shake the foundations of the global economic system. The effect of energy shortages on food production in India and on industrial output in the United States illustrates the link between energy supplies and economic activity.

It is against this backdrop that the energy crisis of the 70's, a crisis of both supply and price, acquires significance. The world is not running out of energy, but oil supplies are shrinking. The world has switched from one energy fuel to another before, but did so gradually and without haste. The shift from wood to coal took several centuries and the more recent substitution of oil for coal was spread over a century. But now the shift from oil to alternative energy sources must be undertaken within the next decade or two. Given the lead times needed to bring new sources of energy into use, there is no time to spare.

The century-long growth in world oil production is projected to reach its zenith and begin to decline within 15 years or so. Oil production in the United States, until recently the world's leading producer, peaked in 1970 and has fallen off steadily since then. The United States was not seriously imperiled by this downturn, since it could fill the widening gap between rising consumption and falling domestic production with imports. The world as a whole obviously will not have this option. It will either turn to alternative energy sources or face the consequences of a shrinking energy supply. While some industrial societies might be able to reduce consumption merely by eliminating waste, countries in which oil is used almost entirely for agricultural and industrial purposes can reduce consumption only by reducing living standards.

Two sets of estimates of world oil reserves—proven reserves (customarily defined as those that can be recovered with current technology and prices) and ultimately recoverable reserves (which allow for new discoveries and for improvements in oil-extraction technology)—can be used to get a rough idea of when oil production will fall off. The estimates of reserves most widely relied upon are those produced by the *Oil and Gas Journal*, which bases its figures on consultation with both governments and oil companies. For 1977 the *Journal* estimated world proven crude oil reserves at 599 billion barrels. Estimates of ultimately recoverable reserves (which are higher than those of proven reserves) have tended over the past decade to range around 2,000 billion barrels.

Most projections now show world oil production peaking in the early 1990's and then steadily declining. As production slows, the growth in demand may substantially outstrip production and lead to severe shortages. Both a U.S. government analysis of the world energy economy and an analysis undertaken by an international group of experts headed by Professor Carroll Wilson at the Massachusetts Institute of Technology suggest that a serious supply-demand imbalance of energy will occur as early as 1981.

Summarizing his group's findings, Professor Wilson said that the world "must drastically curtail the growth of energy use and move massively out of oil into other fuels with wartime urgency" or "face foreseeable catastrophe." He went on to say that the "end of the era of growth in oil production is probably at the most only 15 years away." His findings echoed statements of James R. Schlesinger, Secretary of the U.S. Department of Energy.

The eventual downturn in world oil production will be preceded and hastened by the production decreases in individual countries. The decline already under way in the United States will be followed by downturns in other oil-producing countries. Canada has lost its exportable surplus of oil. Rumania, once a leading oil exporter, is now an importer. The Soviet Union may lose its exportable surplus of oil within a matter of years and leave Eastern Europe entirely dependent on the Middle East and other sources for imports.

The rather abstract global estimates of remaining oil mean more when translated into per capita terms. The upper estimate of 2,000 billion barrels of ultimately recoverable reserves comes to 500 barrels per person for the current world population. An American with a large automobile that averages 10 miles per gallon and that is driven 10,000 miles per year requires just over 20 barrels per year. At this rate, driving alone would exhaust an individual's share of remaining world oil reserves in just 25 years. Besides the assumption that all remaining reserves will be shared equitably, this calculation is based upon the assumptions that all potentially recoverable oil will be economically recovered, that population will not increase further, and that oil will be used only for automotive fuel and not for tractor fuel, petrochemicals, heating, and other purposes.

Nuclear Energy and Coal: New Problems

The end of the age of oil was being contemplated as early as the mid-20th century, but it was no cause for alarm because nuclear power was waiting in the wings along with vast reserves of coal. Yet within a 24-month span between 1975 and 1977, the outlook began to change. In the United States the official projections of nuclear-generated electricity for the end of the century were reduced by two-thirds; an international survey indicated similar reductions in every major Western industrial country. As of mid-1977, for example, West German political parties were contemplating adopting a five-year moratorium on the construction of nuclear power plants.

Efforts to ameliorate the projected downturn in world oil production by turning to nuclear power have brought their own threats to national security. It has not been possible to separate the international spread of nuclear power for peaceful purposes from the spread of bomb-grade nuclear materials. As Denis Hayes notes in *Rays of Hope: The Transition to a Post-Petroleum World,* "widespread weapons proliferation is sure to follow the rapid growth of commercial nuclear power facilities." The modest contribution of nuclear power to the world's energy supplies cannot compensate for the insecurity of a world of present and potential nuclear powers.

Even while the nuclear dream was fading, a respected group

of scientists cautioned against continued heavy reliance on coal. A U.S. National Academy of Sciences study pointed out that use of coal as projected would almost certainly lead to profound and irreversible shifts in the global climatic system. Within two centuries, the Academy foresaw, the burning of coal would lead to a severalfold increase in atmospheric carbon dioxide and an associated rise in the average global temperature of 6°C or 11°F. With oil wells going dry, nuclear power in limbo, and the heavy use of coal threatening to alter the global climate, the urgency of developing renewable energy sources has become obvious.

An Urgent Need

The dominant characteristic of the transition now beginning is this urgency. The time available to make the transition has been shortened by analytical failures, errors in judgment, and a lack of political leadership in the principal industrial countries. At mid-century when it was becoming clear that oil reserves would not last forever, it was mistakenly assumed that nuclear power would fill the void, initially as a source of electrical power and ultimately as a source of other fuels as well. This mistaken assumption led humanity to waste fully a quarter of a century, and now no more than a decade and a half remains before the projected downturn in world oil production.

Even installing solar collectors on individual homes can take a country many years. Hundreds of millions of solar collectors would be needed worldwide by 1990 to offset the projected fall in petroleum production. Technologies must be perfected. Factories must be built to manufacture the solar units. Investment capital must be mobilized. A work force must be trained to install and maintain the collectors. Individual homeowners must be acquainted with solar technologies.

The global transition to renewable energy sources must be made quickly, yet nothing even vaguely resembling a global plan for making this transition has been put on paper. No national timetables, much less a coordinated global timetable for shifting the economy from petroleum to renewable energy sources, have been drafted. The rate of transition from petroleum to solar energy sources, the number of solar collectors to be installed each year by country, the number of windmills to be erected where wind power is economically feasible, and the area of farmland to be devoted to the various energy crops all need to be calculated.

Circumstances suggest the need for a crash energy conservation program and for a broad-based global effort to develop the entire range of renewable energy sources. An all-out conservation program is needed to stretch remaining oil reserves as far as possible and so buy time to shift to renewable energy sources. The challenge is to husband scarce petroleum resources while designing a sustainable and petroleum-free economic system.

Inexhaustible energy: Sunlight, focused by mirror array onto a tower-top boiler, will drive a 10,000-kilowatt steam-turbine generator in this McDonnell Douglas design. Pilot model is planned for California's sunny Mojave Desert.

McDonnell Douglas Astronautics Company

The risk is that petroleum supplies will be squandered frivolously on nonessential uses before an economic system can be developed that is not dependent on oil.

The need for all the countries of the world to act in concert to formulate and launch a transition program, including devising a timetable, is paramount. But only a few countries such as China—with its methane generators, small-scale hydroelectric generators, and reforestation programs—and Brazil—with its ethanol automotive-fuel program—are systematically developing their renewable energy sources.

Without a timetable, the world may one day discover that most of its oil and gas is gone and that alternative sources of energy are not adequate to sustain the economic system. Denis Hayes believes that the energy transition will require a global mobilization of resources comparable to that for World War II. In his spring 1977 energy message, President Jimmy Carter likened the energy situation to "the moral equivalent of war." The President's assessment would have been even grimmer had he awaited the National Academy of Sciences study of energy and climate, which indicates the dangers to climate of long-term reliance on coal.

4

Deteriorating Biological Systems

Pressures on the earth's principal biological systems are mounting rapidly as population expands and as incomes climb. Stress is evident in each of the four major biological systems—oceanic fisheries, grasslands, forests and croplands—on which humanity depends for food and industrial raw materials. Except for croplands, all are essentially natural systems, little modified by humans. Tree farming and fish farming offer a means of expanding output beyond that of the natural systems, but this requires additional energy.

Discussions of long-term economic growth prospects in recent years have concentrated on nonrenewable resources, especially minerals and fossil fuels. They have been undergirded by the implicit assumption that because biological resources are renewable, they are of little concern. In fact, both the nonrenewable and renewable resource bases have been shrinking. In addition to food, biological systems provide virtually all the raw materials for industry except petroleum-derived synthetics and minerals such as iron ore, bauxite and copper.

The current world population of 4 billion humans is putting great pressure on these biological systems, often more than they can endure over the long term. The productivity of scores of oceanic fisheries is falling as the catch exceeds their regenerative capacities. In a protein-hungry world, overfishing has recently

The Soviet Union, with 260 million mouths to feed and a chronic food deficit, sends trawlers to all world fishing grounds including New England—where U.S. Coast Guard planes watch for overfishing.

Wide World Photos

become the rule, not the exception. Forests are shrinking before the onslaught of the firewood gatherer, the land-hungry farmer, and the international timber interests.

As numbers of cattle, water buffalo, sheep, goats and camels increase along with human populations, the earth's grasslands are being overtaxed. Denudation, soil erosion and desert encroachment result. Croplands also are under pressure, and frontiers have largely disappeared. Fallow cycles everywhere are shortening.

Fisheries, Grasslands and Forests

The oceanic food chain, yielding some 70 million tons of fish per year, is humanity's principal source of high-quality protein. Not only do fish provide animal protein for direct consumption, but the less palatable species are converted into fish meal and fed to poultry that produce meat and eggs. Fisheries also yield fish oil and other specialized by-products used by industry.

Throughout most of human history, there were far more fish in the oceans than we could ever hope to catch. This perceived abundance led to an enormous expansion of world fishing fleets during the period since World War II. Investment in fishing capacity increased severalfold as the industry adopted sophisticated technologies such as fish-tracking using sonar. Between

1950 and 1970, the catch increased by an average of nearly 5 percent yearly, far outstripping population growth and sharply boosting per capita supplies of marine protein. During this two-decade span, the catch more than tripled, climbing from 21 million to 70 million metric tons. At nearly 70 million tons in live weight, it averaged some 40 pounds per person annually, well above the annual offtake from the world's beef herds.

Between 1950 and 1970, fish supplied a steadily expanding share of human protein needs, but in 1970 the trend was abruptly and unexpectedly interrupted. Since then, the catch has fluctuated between 65 million and 70 million tons, clouding the prospects for an ever-bigger catch. Meanwhile, world population growth has led to an 11 percent decline in the per capita catch and to rising prices for virtually every edible species.

The earth's grasslands too are under growing pressure. The products originating from the 6 billion acres of grassland play an important role in the food, energy and industrial sectors of the global economy. Grasslands supply many protein foods, several forms of energy, and numerous raw materials for industry.

Grasslands support the ruminants that supply most of the world's meat, milk, butter and cheese. In addition to protein for human consumption, they provide energy for agriculture. Just as the firewood from forests serves as fuel for cooking, so grasslands supply the energy for the draft animals that till a third of the world's croplands.

The one-fifth of the earth's land surface on which forage for ruminants and other animals is produced is a cornerstone of the global economy. Integral parts of both the world food and the world energy economies, these grasslands and the 2.7 billion domesticated ruminants they support—1.2 billion cattle, 1 billion sheep, 400 million goats, and 130 million water buffalo—also represent an essential source of raw materials for industry. Their production potential and their condition directly influence the prospects of feeding our still-expanding population. As humanity's demand for meat, milk, butter, cheese, leather, tallow and wool has risen over the past generation, pressures on grasslands have increased markedly. So, too, has the need for more draft animals intensified the pressure on grasslands. But in some areas, supporting existing populations of draft animals has already become well-nigh impossible, and draft animals too emaciated to draw plows are becoming common sights. Now that the hope of replacing water buffalo or bullocks with tractors has been deferred by the oil shortage in many poor countries, overgrazing both directly threatens the supply of livestock products and, by weakening draft animals, indirectly threatens food production.

Overgrazing is not new, but its scale and rate of acceleration are unprecedented. Deterioration that once took centuries is now being compressed into years by inexorable population growth. Populations are, in effect, outgrowing the biological systems that sustain them.

Destruction of forests in Pakistan has eroded soil, silted rivers and reduced wood yield. Scientific forest management is one aim of UN technical aid.

United Nations

Humanity depends on the earth's forests for firewood, lumber, newsprint, and a host of less essential products. Wood pulp is the raw material used in the manufacture of rayon. Paper is the feedstock of modern industrial societies, in which more people are employed in offices than in factories or on farms. In a bureaucratic, nonindustrial city like Washington, it is the principal raw material. It is the common medium of both mass and interpersonal communication everywhere.

Firewood is still the principal energy fuel in many "third world" countries. Villagers in the poor countries where firewood is used for cooking are decimating local forests. The average villager requires nearly a ton of firewood each year, and expanding village populations are raising firewood demands so fast that the regenerative capacities of many forests are being surpassed. Forests recede farther and farther from the villages until entire regions and countries are eventually deforested.

While firewood is a principal energy source only in developing countries, wood is a primary building material everywhere. Vast tracts of forests are cut to secure the lumber used to build houses, schools, churches, offices, shops, bridges, railroads, factories and storage facilities. But even though the forests are being decimated, most of humanity is poorly housed: the need to house some 64 million new inhabitants each year, coupled with the need to replace existing housing, is raising total claims on many remaining forests beyond a sustainable level.

A third major pressure on the earth's woodlands comes from the demand for newsprint. As the share of humanity that is literate expands, the demand for newsprint expands even more rapidly than population. The pressures of these rising demands are further aggravated by a lack of paper-recycling facilities in principal paper-consuming countries.

Forests have proved to be one of humanity's most valuable economic resources and, in consequence, to be one of the most heavily exploited. Almost every country undergoing rapid population growth is being deforested. If cutting is excessive, forests shrink and their capacity to satisfy human needs diminishes. Most of the Middle East and North Africa and much

United Nations

Ruined croplands are typified by this scene in Sahelian (semidesert) region of Senegal, where a student farmer plows the sand.

of continental Asia, Central America, and the Andean regions of South America are now virtually treeless. In these denuded areas, wood and wood products are scarce and expensive. What is worse, the remaining forested area in all these regions except eastern Asia, principally China, is shrinking.

Croplands and Soil Erosion

Croplands produce an even greater variety of products. They supply food, industrial raw materials such as rubber, and a variety of fibers, alcohols, starches and vegetable oils. The proportionate contribution of cultivated crops to the global economy is far greater than the one-tenth of the earth's land surface that they occupy.

As world population gradually expanded after the development of agriculture, farming spread from valley to valley and from continent to continent until by the mid-20th century the frontiers had virtually disappeared. Even while the amount of new land awaiting the plow shrank, the growth in demand for food was expanding at a record pace. Coupled with the uneven distribution of land in many countries, these trends have engendered a land hunger that is driving millions of farmers onto soils of marginal quality—lands subject to low and unreliable rainfall, lands with inherently low fertility, lands too steep to sustain cultivation.

Anyone who has traveled across Africa, up and down the Indian subcontinent, or around Latin America has seen firsthand the consequences of extending cultivation onto land that should either be left in its natural state or cultivated only with special techniques. One need be neither a trained agronomist nor a prophet to see the grim future in store if the abuse of the earth's meager soil resources continues.

Apart from the loss of cropland, erosion on remaining cropland is undermining soil productivity. A natural process, soil erosion as such is neither new nor necessarily alarming, but when erosion outpaces the formation of new soil, inherent soil fertility declines.

The mantle of topsoil covering the earth ranges in depth from a few inches to a few hundred feet. Over much of the earth's surface it is only inches deep, usually less than a foot. Nature produces new soil very slowly, much more slowly than the rate at which humans are now removing it. Thus, once topsoil is lost, a vital capacity to sustain life is diminished. With soil as with many other resources, humanity is beginning to ask more of the earth than it can give.

It is the rate of soil erosion that distinguishes the current era from other periods. In vast areas, the amount of topsoil that is being lost through erosion exceeds that being formed by nature. Soil scientists analyzing the relationship between soil loss and formation have established a tolerable rate of soil loss (T factor). This T factor ordinarily varies from one to five tons per acre, depending on the local conditions. In a survey of Wisconsin soils, 70 percent experienced soil losses greater than the tolerable levels; on soils with a T factor of 3.6 tons, the actual loss was 8.4 tons, more than double the tolerable rate.

Concern over the loss of topsoil in the United States is escalating. Luther Carter writes in *Science* that "the erosion of croplands by wind and water remains one of the biggest, most pervasive problems the nation faces." The problem persists because, "in the calculations of many farmers, the hope of maximizing short-term crop yields and profits has taken precedence over the longer-term advantages of conserving the soil." In an analysis of the condition of U.S. soils, the Iowa-based Council for Agricultural Science and Technology reports that "a third of all cropland was suffering soil losses too great to be sustained without a gradual, but ultimately disastrous, decline in productivity." U.S. Secretary of Agriculture Bob Bergland has called for a new research effort to determine more fully the extent of U.S. soil deterioration. He is well aware that even the heavy use of fertilizer cannot over the longer term suffice to compensate for losses beyond a certain point.

Biological Limits: Challenge to Diplomacy

More and more the "carrying capacities" of biological systems are being ignored and exceeded. In many ways the natural biological systems on which humanity depends function like a philanthropic foundation operating on a fixed endowment. With $100 million that earns 6 percent yearly, a foundation can safely disburse $6 million per year indefinitely. If, however,

Exhaustion of cropland produced this erosion in cassava-growing valley of East Java, Indonesia. UN Food and Agriculture Organization aid is designed to promote better land use in the area.

United Nations

overly enthusiastic project officers begin disbursing the foundation's resources at $10 million per year, the foundation's financial assets would gradually be consumed. Eventually, the foundation would lose its productive assets and close its doors. So, too, with biological systems. In neither case can the offtake exceed the regenerative capacity for long.

In many third world countries population growth is now acting as a double-edged sword, simultaneously expanding demands on the biological systems while destroying the resource bases. As long as the demand for fish is less than the sustainable yield of the fishery, population growth has no impact on production. But once the demand exceeds the sustainable yield, then population growth begins to eat away the productive resource base. In some cases, this process can continue until the biological resource is entirely destroyed.

History has recorded a few instances of such abuse. North Africa was once the granary of the Roman Empire. Today, the fertility of the region's badly eroded soils has fallen so low that the area imports most of its food. Accounts of the collapse of the early Middle Eastern civilizations attributed the downfall of these societies to invaders from the north, but more recent investigations link their decline to the waterlogging and salting of their irrigation systems and to the collapse of their food supplies. For some countries, encroaching deserts pose a far greater threat than invading armies.

Efforts to preserve the biological systems on which humanity depends must ultimately involve constraints on global consumption. Negotiating limits on the consumption of tuna or newsprint will bring national interests into conflict, putting great pressure on the international political system. Resolving such problems will tax the skills of diplomats.

5
Climate Modification

Climate and climate change have always influenced human social evolution, but only recently have humans acquired the means to influence climate. Usually inadvertent, the human influence on climate can sharply reduce food production, and hence a country's security. In low-income countries unable to offset crop shortfalls with imports, a production drop can translate directly into a rise in death rates.

As a 1975 study by the National Academy of Sciences reports, "While the natural variations of climate have been larger than those that may have been induced by human activities during the past century, the rapidity with which human impacts threaten to grow in the future, and increasingly to disturb the natural course of events, is a matter of concern." The Academy study went on to note that "these impacts include man's changes of the atmospheric composition and his direct interference with factors controlling the all-important heat balance."

The earth's heat budget equals the amount of energy it receives from the sun minus the amount reflected or radiated into space. If this delicate balance were altered so that the earth retained more or less heat than it had in the past, the earth's climate would change. If it retained much less, a new ice age would begin. If it retained a great deal more, the polar ice caps would melt—raising the oceans and submerging vast tracts of land and coastal cities.

Wide World Photos

Fossil fuels, burned at record rates in 20th century, simultaneously warm the atmosphere with carbon dioxide and cool it with dust. Net effect on world climate is still uncertain.

The earth's absorption and reflection of heat can be altered in many ways. At the local level, the shift from forest to field altered this capacity, as did that from field to desert. The deforestation of vast areas, either as a result of clearing land for agriculture or of cutting firewood, can influence local climates measurably. Conducted on a large enough scale, deforestation could change the global climate as well.

Are We Heating the Earth . . .

The chief worry emerging among the meteorologists and geophysicists who study the earth's heat balance is that increases in the amount of carbon dioxide in the atmosphere will promote a "green-house effect." Carbon dioxide (CO_2) does not reduce incoming solar radiation but it does absorb some of the heat that is reradiated. Thus, any atmospheric rise in the CO_2 level would cause the atmospheric temperature to increase.

At present, vast tonnages of carbon that have been sealed under the earth in fossil fuels for geological epochs are being released into the atmosphere. Since the beginning of the industrial revolution, the burning of fossil fuels has raised CO_2 levels in the atmosphere by an estimated 13 percent, and, as a 1977 study by the National Academy of Sciences projects, a four- to eight-fold increase in atmospheric carbon dioxide can be expected within the next two centuries if the present heavy reliance on fossil fuels continues. According to the Academy study, "our best understanding of the relation between an increase in carbon dioxide in the atmosphere and change in global temperature suggests a corresponding increase in average world temperature of 6°C or more with polar temperature increases of as much as three times this figure."

This increase in average temperature of 6°C or 11°F would be accompanied by increases in humidity and in precipitation. If the temperature rise led to even a 5°C warming of the upper 1,000 meters of ocean water, simple expansion would raise the sea level by about one meter. In the preface to the Academy study, Philip Abelson and Thomas Malone indicate that "the primary limiting factor on energy production from fossil fuels over the next few centuries may turn out to be the climatic effects of the release of carbon dioxide." They then report that averting a wholesale warming of the earth "will require a carefully planned international program and a fine sense of timing on the part of decision-makers."

The amount of fossil fuels that can be safely burned over the long term may be determined more by the effect of their combustion on climate than by any other factor. Apart from the air pollution associated with burning fossil fuels, the carbon dioxide factor may force the world to shift to solar energy sources. The direct use of sunlight, wind power and water power does not raise atmospheric CO_2 levels. Nor does the burning of wood unless it contributes to net deforestation.

Another source of climatic change is thermal pollution, as weather forecasts for major cities remind us daily. Temperature levels recorded within the inner city are commonly several degrees higher than those of the outlying areas. So far, the clearly measurable thermal effects remain largely localized, but continuing growth in fossil-fuel use could eventually lead to global temperature increases. A 1977 Ford Foundation sponsored study, *Nuclear Power: Issues and Choices,* reported that electric power generation can both directly and indirectly warm up the earth. "The thermal output of both coal and nuclear power plants contributes directly to the long-term heating of the atmosphere. A much more immediate atmospheric heating problem, however, results from the carbon dioxide produced when coal is burned."

...Or Cooling It?

Another potential influence on climate is that of airborne dust, the most common and easily recognized of the man-made pollutants that affect climate. Dust is generated by virtually every human activity from suburban driving to tilling the soil. Meteorologist Helmut Landsberg estimates that, along with world population, the amount of dust in the atmosphere has doubled since the 30's despite the absence of major volcanic eruptions. Other sources estimate that the amount of dust or particulate matter being discharged into the atmosphere is now increasing by about 4 percent per year. At this rate of increase, dust levels at the close of the century would climb far beyond present levels. Since particulate matter in the atmosphere tends to scatter incoming radiation and to reflect it back into space before it reaches earth, particles form what amounts to a layer of insulation, reflecting the sun's rays away from the earth and thereby lowering the planet's temperature. The combined effect of this cooling process and the warming processes described above is not yet fully understood, and requires further research.

Apart from the inadvertent modification of climate, deliberate attempts to alter the climate are becoming increasingly common. Chief among these are efforts to increase rainfall where water supplies are inadequate. Some rainmaking technologies have proven at least moderately successful. In fact, the issue of cloud-seeding precipitated a clash in the United States between the states of Washington and Idaho during the drought-ridden early months of 1977. Washington's state officials, who had hired a rainmaking firm to seed clouds moving inland from the Pacific, were accused by Idaho's political leaders of "cloud rustling." This relatively tame skirmish raises the prospect of meteorological warfare as countries that are hard-pressed to expand food supplies begin to compete for available rainfall.

That humans can inadvertently or intentionally alter global climatic patterns is now beyond doubt. Whether the world would be "better" if it were warmer or cooler is a moot question: existing agricultural systems and settlement patterns have evolved in a particular climate, and climatic changes of any sort can only disrupt those systems. Even an average temperature decline of one degree in the northern latitudes could reduce the growing season by two weeks. Even minor reductions in temperatures in the northern hemisphere could lead to a southward shift of the monsoon belt in both Africa and Asia. In either case, agricultural output would shrink, adversely affecting the well-being and survival prospects of hundreds of millions of people.

6
Global Food Insecurity

The world food economy has undergone a basic transformation during the 70's. Not only did the world have huge surplus stocks and excess production capacity at the beginning of the decade, but it also appeared that both would be long-lived. Some 50 million acres out of a total U.S. cropland base of 350 million acres was held out of production to support prices. Together grain stockpiles and the U.S. cropland reserve provided security for all humankind, a cushion against any imaginable food disasters. Suddenly in 1972 and 1973, they both disappeared, and the whole world began struggling to make it from one harvest to the next. Global food insecurity became greater than at any time since the years immediately following World War II.

Although grain stocks have been partially rebuilt in the late 70's, the global balance between the supply and demand for food remains delicate, as the extreme sensitivity of commodity prices to weather reports indicates. The forecast of rain in western Kansas can send wheat-futures prices down the daily limit on the Chicago Board of Trade. A report that the Indian monsoon has started three weeks later than usual can send wheat prices up the limit. When the balance of supply and demand is so precarious, a crop shortfall in a major producing country can set off a wave of global inflation. In poor countries,

Chicago Board of Trade, world's biggest grain market, reacted frantically to news of huge secret Soviet grain deal in 1972.

Wide World Photos

where rising food prices can push death rates upward, a crop failure can also have a demographic impact.

Most of the factors contributing to the transformation of the world food economy are inherent in efforts to expand food production in a world where some food-producing systems are under stress, where returns on some agricultural inputs are diminishing, and where land is inequitably distributed. Systemic stresses are reflected in the decline of the fish catch, the encroachment of deserts on farmland, widespread soil erosion (especially in third world countries) and the growing difficulties attending the further expansion of both the cropped area and the irrigated area.

1972: The Shock of Food Scarcity

As recently as early 1972, the dual reserve of grain and idled cropland seemed more than adequate for the foreseeable future, but then the growth in global demand for food began to outstrip production. Adverse weather brought the longer-term deterioration in the food situation into public view much as the Organization of Petroleum Exporting Countries (OPEC) price rise brought the precariousness of the energy situation into sight.

In 1961, the combination of reserve grain stocks in exporting countries and the production equivalent of the idled U.S. cropland equaled 112 days of world grain consumption. (See Figure 1.) In 1969 the same combination totaled 93 days. Shortly thereafter it began to fall—to 60 days in 1972 and still further to

39 days in 1973. All of the idled cropland was released for production by 1974, entirely eliminating this reserve.

In 1976, the rarity of simultaneous record grain harvests in three of four leading food-producing countries—the United States, the Soviet Union and India—led to modest stock rebuilding. An unusually good worldwide harvest in 1977 further contributed to stock rebuilding, raising reserves to the equivalent of 54 days of consumption for 1978. But even this exceedingly encouraging development guarantees only a minimal level of food security. Far less than the margin of 90 to 110 days that prevailed in the early 1960's, the world's food stocks are even less than those held in 1972, which poor harvests in the Soviet Union, India and a number of smaller countries wiped out in less than two years.

Throughout the postwar period, the food situation in most

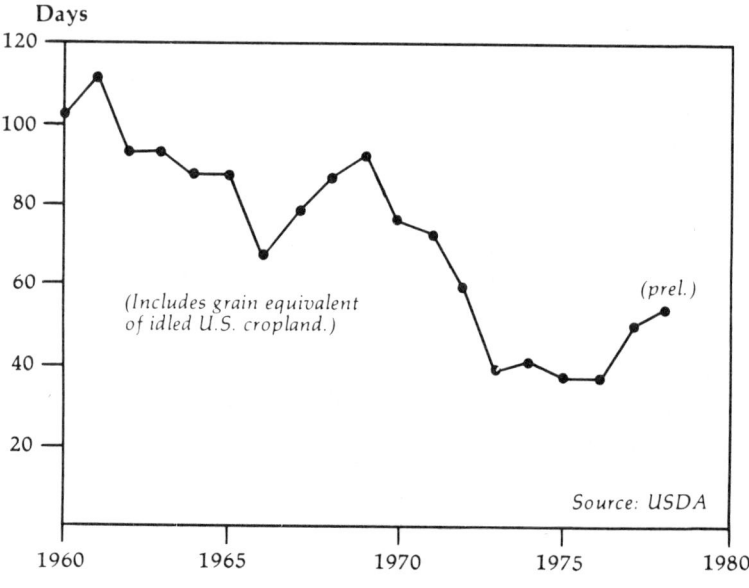

Figure 1: World Grain Reserves as Days of World Consumption, 1960–78

third world countries had gradually improved. From the end of World War II, improvements in per capita food consumption and nutrition led to a decline in death rates. Indeed, all was going well until the early 70's when this trend of gradual improvement was interrupted. Both the world per capita fish catch and the per capita production of food then began to decline. So, too, did food reserves, as the consumption of food began to outpace production. Food security declined to a postwar low in 1973 and remained at a precariously low level for four years. The international community, stripped of its reserves, was no longer able to respond effectively to crop shortages in individual countries. This period contrasted sharply with the 50's and 60's, when the United States was prepared to intervene with food-aid shipments whenever and wherever famine threatened. After consecutive monsoon failures in 1965 and 1966, for instance, the United States shipped a fifth of its wheat crop to India two years in a row and helped that country avert widespread famine.

The food scarcity and soaring prices of the 70's affected all countries, but, as we saw in chapter 2, the brunt of the crisis was borne by the poorest countries which, to make matters worse, must support rapidly growing populations. Thus Bangladesh, in two bad harvest years, lost an estimated 700,000 people to hunger—far more than the combat losses in the 1971–72 Bangladesh war. India's crop failure in 1972 cost far more lives than the combat fatalities in any war since World War II. Africa's death from starvation and related causes in the Sahelian and Ethiopian-Somali regions during the 70's may proportionately outweigh Asia's.

India, too, was hard hit during the 70's. After a poor harvest in 1972, the Indian government discovered that the Soviet Union had tied up most of the world's exportable wheat supplies, leaving little for India to use to offset its poor harvest. Thus, the Indian government sat by helplessly while food consumption fell and death rates climbed. In the three poorest states of Uttar Pradesh, Bihar and Orissa, the increase in death rates above the previous year represented an estimated 829,000 lives. The loss of life in India alone far exceeded the combat fatalities which were suffered in any war since World War II.

Hunger has also taken a grim toll in Africa during the current decade; there, the proportionate loss may outweigh Asia's. A prolonged drought in Sahelian Africa has brought the deteriorating food situation there into sharp focus. The six countries of the Sahelian zone—Senegal, Mauritania, Niger, Upper Volta, Chad and Mali—all suffered loss of life. But no one knows exactly how many died. Cornell nutritionist Professor Michael Latham testified before the U.S. Congress that the number of lives lost was probably somewhere between 100,000 and 250,000.

Causes of the Food Crisis

Several factors have contributed to the global food insecurity of the 70's. One of the most dramatic was the political decision by the Soviet government to admit publicly the shortcomings of its agriculture rather than impose food rationing. When the Soviet government turned to the world food market with the largest food deficit of any country in history, it discovered that no country or combination of countries other than the United States could satisfy its needs. A Republican Administration in Washington responded enthusiastically to the Soviet need, virtually emptying U.S. grain bins in the process. In responding as it did, the United States assumed the responsibility for feeding its principal political and military adversary, one against whom the lion's share of the $104 billion defense budget was directed.

The Soviet Union is not the only Eastern European country heavily dependent on Western food. Poland, East Germany and Czechoslovakia are regular customers. Without cheap food from the West to augment its domestic food supplies, the Polish government might well have fallen during the summer of 1976—when riots in the principal cities forced the government to roll back food price increases.

Rapid population growth, as Chapter 2 showed, has also emerged as an enormous factor in the food insecurity of the 70's. Virtually all countries with falling per capita food output are those with populations increasing at the rate of 15- to 20-fold per century. The record global growth in demand for food, for some 30 million additional tons of grain per year in good weather or bad, is fueled both by the unyielding growth of population and by growing affluence, with the former accounting for two-thirds or more of the annual growth.

Closely related to the contribution of population growth to food insecurity in the third world is a complex of negative ecological trends—deforestation, overgrazing, desert encroachment, soil erosion and flooding. Pakistan, with rivers originating in the western Himalayas, has experienced the worst flooding in its history. A foreign ambassador in Addis Ababa described the effect of soil erosion in Ethiopia rather graphically when he said that the country is quite "literally going down the river." Arthur Candell, writing of the ecological undermining of the Haitian economy, reports that "the land produces less and less each year, while population soars. . . . The eroded and leached mountain soil can no longer support tree growth."

Similarly, the flood which heavily damaged the rice crop in Bangladesh in 1974-75—among the most severe on record—was perhaps due as much to the hand of man as to that of nature. In large measure it was the product of the extensive deforestation of the watersheds in Nepal and eastern India, where two of Bangladesh's principal rivers originate.

Unfortunately, many of the third world countries plagued with rapid population growth have managed agriculture poorly. Social forces that have concentrated landholdings in the hands of a few have crowded a majority of the farm population onto a small area of land, or even worse, off the land entirely. Consequently, both land and labor are grossly underutilized. In country after country, continuing malnutrition and growing national food deficits are due more to existing social structures than to a lack of productive capacity.

Often two or more of the above factors operate together. Some countries are confronted simultaneously with rapid population growth, ecological deterioration of the food system, and agricultural mismanagement. Among these are Algeria and Iran, where per capita grain production has fallen over the past

Wide World Photos

With world food stocks low and much of mankind malnourished, 1977 drought in the world's principal granary, the American Midwest, carried global implications.

quarter-century by 61 and 42 percent, respectively. This same combination of factors has forced other countries, such as Libya and Venezuela, to import half of their total grain supply.

The Outlook: Hunger and Instability

Since World War II every continent except North America has become food-deficient. Indeed, those countries with significant exportable surpluses can be numbered on the fingers of one hand. In response to growing food deficits around the world, the U.S. and Canada increased their grain exports from 56 million tons in 1970 to 94 million tons in 1976. Since the United States and Canada experience the same climatic cycles, this overwhelming dependence on one geographic region also contributes to the global food insecurity.

The current decade has witnessed the depletion of world food reserves, the repeated restriction of exports by the principal suppliers, record food prices worldwide, and hunger-induced rises in death rates in at least a dozen countries. As the decade draws to a close, the international community must at least prepare for the possibility that the food scramble of recent years may not be temporary. The slack appears to have gone out of the world food economy, leaving the entire world in a highly vulnerable position.

Unless countries can give agriculture the financial and scientific support it needs, hunger-induced rises in death rates will probably continue to claim far more lives than military conflict. It is also quite possible that food scarcities and soaring food prices may contribute more than any other factor to political instability. In some cases, the change in government will come via the ballot box. In others it will come through less peaceful means.

7

Economic Threats to Security

Economically, the 70's have been traumatic and confusing. They have brought the first global double-digit inflation on record during peacetime and the highest unemployment since the Great Depression. Capital shortages are plaguing the citadels of capitalism and socialism alike. This unexplained coexistence of inflation and unemployment has led to a situation for which economists cannot prescribe a satisfactory remedy.

Global Inflation

Inflation is as old as money. But its global character and some of its recent causes are fairly new on the scene. Historically, inflation has been a localized phenomenon, ravaging individual countries from time to time. But during the 70's, it has assumed a global dimension, affecting countries everywhere. The meshing of the economic cycles of virtually all the major industrial countries in the mid-70's contributed both to inflation's spread and to its record severity. With virtually all the industrial economies simultaneously on the upswing, the worldwide demand for both raw materials and manufactured goods expanded at a record rate. The virulent inflation that ensued affected even the inflation-resistant United States, financially conservative Switzerland, and socialist Poland (which had clung to the belief that socialism was somehow immune to inflationary forces).

Although global double-digit inflation is unique to the 70's, it has been many years in the making. Throughout the postwar period the average rise in price levels in the Organization for Economic Cooperation and Development (OECD) countries, which account for the bulk of the world's output of goods and services, has been gradually accelerating. From 1953 to 1960, the annual rate of inflation in the OECD countries was 2.3 percent. During the first half of the 60's it increased to 3.9 percent. By 1970 it was running at 5.5 percent. In 1971 it increased further to 6.3 percent, and by early 1974 it had surpassed 10 percent.

Although the prices of many commodities have climbed abruptly, the fourfold increase in the price of oil thus far during this decade is perhaps the most dramatic and foreboding hike. These steep rises in petroleum prices reflected OPEC's decision to "administer" prices, but the strength to make its resolution stick derived from the lack of suitable substitutes for oil.

The prices of nonrenewable and renewable resources have both increased during the 70's. The world price of wheat, for example, tripled between 1970 and 1974. Although the big jump in prices followed the massive Soviet purchase of U.S. wheat during the summer of 1972, the Soviet purchase was merely the triggering event that brought the longer-term trends into focus. The growth in world demand for food during the early 70's simply outstripped the capacity of farmers to expand supplies of wheat and other commodities at historical price levels.

Matching the rises in the prices of food staples such as wheat was an equally dramatic rise in the price of soybeans, a principal source of high quality protein. Between 1970 and 1973, world soybean prices increased two-and-one-half times, and during the four years since they have shown no indication of returning to the remarkably stable level that prevailed before 1971. The soaring price of soybeans reflects both the inability of agricultural scientists to raise soybean yields significantly and a worldwide scarcity of land on which to produce soybeans. Moreover, the deterioration of oceanic fisheries places additional pressures on soybeans and other land-based protein sources.

Like soybean prices, the prices of lumber and firewood have doubled and in some cases tripled during the 70's. Between 1970 and 1976, newsprint increased in price from about $150 per ton to just under $300 per ton. Although the sharp climb was commonly attributed to the global surge in economic expansion of the early 70's, the subsequent cessation of economic growth during the mid-70's did not bring prices down. The "ratchet effect" that seems to be operating here suggests strongly that it is the overall relationship between the level of demand and the sustainable yield of forests—and not the short-term shift in demand—that counts.

Even things normally taken for granted, such as land, living space, fresh water, and clean air, become costly in a crowded, increasingly affluent world. Land prices required for home building have soared everywhere. Between 1966 and 1976, the average price for a new home in the United States climbed from just under $30,000 to just over $50,000.

Severe inflation can distort both economic and social values. It rewards speculators and penalizes savers. It can wipe out lifetime savings almost overnight or reduce people on low or fixed income to unexpected penury. Its impact on different groups within a society is invariably uneven. Those who suffer most often protest, as they did in Colombia in September of 1977, when workers struck and demanded pay raises to match the 29 percent inflation rate. *The New York Times* described the situation as the strike turned violent: "Rioting in the slums of Bogotá killed at least 6 more persons today, bringing the death toll to 16. Thousands of troops in battle gear patrolled the city in jeeps and armored cars." If global inflationary forces are not managed more effectively such incidents could become commonplace.

Inflationary stresses can quickly aggravate social divisions, turning political cracks into fissures. Perhaps the ultimate threat of uncontrolled inflation is that it eventually undermines public confidence in governments and institutions and can thus pave

Combination of rapid inflation and a government wage freeze led to violence in Bogotá, Colombia, in September 1977.

the way for violent shifts to the radical right or left. When Helmut Schmidt, now West German chancellor, was finance minister in early 1974, he voiced his concern: "I only have to go to the years 1931 to 1933 to say that the meaning of stability is not limited to prices."

Global Unemployment

Efforts to cope with inflation by slowing economic growth have aggravated another economic ill—rising unemployment. The global labor force is growing at a record rate. Young people are flooding the labor market in the poor countries, and ever more women of all ages are entering the job market in the rich ones. Governments have become accustomed to creating additional jobs by promoting overall economic growth, and in some countries this growth long outran the indigenous labor supply. Acute labor shortages plagued northwestern Europe and Japan during the 60's and early 70's as the number of jobs created by record economic expansion outstripped the number of new entrants into the job market. However, by the mid-70's rising unemployment had even these countries in its grip.

If new employment is to be created, there must be something for people to work with. For the half or so of the global labor force in agriculture, that "something" is land. From the age of exploration onward, the jobless have moved to the frontiers of human settlement and have often been able to obtain land there for the asking. In fact, this centrifugal force long saved Europe from the throes of overpopulation. As long as frontiers existed, employment could be created with trifling amounts of capital—with that needed to buy crude farm implements and seed. But

Many "sodbusters" who opened the Great Plains to farming, as in this Nebraska scene in 1887, came from land-hungry Europe. Disappearance of such frontiers sharpens today's food crisis.

Wide World Photos

now that land suitable for settlement has become scarce or concentrated in a few hands, new agricultural jobs cannot be readily created unless land is redistributed.

As the opportunities for continuing rapid economic growth subside, unemployment spreads. During the recession of the mid-70's some 17 million workers, the highest number in 40 years, were unemployed in North America, Japan, and in the industrial countries of Western Europe. Supplying this continuously expanding corps of jobless with unemployment benefits and welfare payments is becoming a serious burden. In many poor countries, entrants into the job market outnumber new jobs by two to one; levels of unemployment in these countries are without precedent.

India's labor force was projected to increase from 210 million to 273 million during the 70's. Although the nation is already stricken with widespread unemployment and underemployment, 100,000 new entrants join the Indian labor force each week. According to the estimates of economist Harry T. Oshima, at least 15 percent of the labor force is unemployed in Pakistan, Sri Lanka, Malaysia and the Philippines. One-third of Bangladesh's available manpower may be unemployed. Indonesia's working-age population is growing by an estimated 1.8 million annually; one-fourth of its potential labor force may now be jobless. Data for scores of other countries show the same common trend.

Looking at the developing countries as a whole, the International Labour Office (ILO) estimated that 24.7 percent of the total labor force was either out of work or underemployed in 1970. The comparable figure for 1980 is expected to approach 30 percent. Between 1970 and the end of the century, the labor force in the less-developed countries is projected by the ILO to expand by 91 percent. To accommodate such expansion, a phenomenal 922 million additional jobs would have to be created. The projected growth in the developed countries, meanwhile, will be only 33 percent.

In countries with low fertility rates, young people entering the labor markets step into vacancies created by the retirement of

United Press International

Low-paid Mexican *braceros*, **picking California strawberries, typify world tide of job-seekers migrating from poor nations.**

older workers. In countries with high fertility rates, comparatively few older workers retire each year while large numbers of the young annually join the lines for jobs. Consequently, half to two-thirds of all new entrants into the job market in the third world require newly created jobs.

If ILO projections prove accurate, the world labor force will increase from 1.51 billion in 1970 to 2.58 billion by the year 2000. Employing 35 million more people per year in productive ways will require vast amounts of capital and natural resources, including energy.

One consequence of the inability of governments in countries with rapid population growth to create sufficient jobs is massive emigration to countries with slower population growth rates and, hence, more available jobs. The quest for jobs is driving people across national borders in ever-growing numbers. Today, the United States is home for 8 million to 12 million illegal migrants, at least 6 million of them believed to be Mexican. Each day thousands of additional Mexicans cross the U.S. border, making a mockery of passports, visas and immigration laws.

In an earlier era, unlicensed workers were seized by immigration authorities and deported. Today the numbers have overwhelmed the staff and resources of the Immigration and Naturalization Service. The blunt fact is that U.S. borders are no longer secure. Emigration does not solve unemployment problems if those emigrating enter countries where unemployment is already substantial. The net effect of illegal Mexican migration into the United States is to shift unemployment from rural Mexico to urban America. Indeed, the number of aliens believed to be holding jobs in the United States in 1977 approximated 6 million—the number of Americans out of work and actively seeking jobs. Illegal immigrants not only compete with Americans for jobs; they also often collect welfare payments, adding to the burden of financially troubled cities such as New York.

In Europe, a legal migration of workers on a comparable scale has occurred between the preindustrial countries surrounding the Mediterranean and the industrial countries of northwestern Europe. As economic growth rates accelerated in Western Europe following World War II, labor shortages developed. Among other governments, those of France, Germany, the Netherlands, Switzerland and Belgium began to invite workers from Mediterranean countries to work for an unspecified period of time. These southerners were clearly not being invited to apply for citizenship, but rather to remain in the host countries as "guest" workers. Not surprisingly, invitations to countries where wages were low and jobs were scarce brought guest workers in droves. By the early 70's the migrants in Western Europe from countries such as Turkey, Yugoslavia, Algeria, Italy, Spain, Portugal, Morocco, Tunisia and Greece numbered an estimated 10 million to 11 million, equaling the combined population of Denmark and Ireland. In individual countries, they made up anywhere from one-twentieth to one-third of the labor force.

Since the postwar boom, dramatic changes have occurred. The severe economic downturn of the mid-70's made fully employing even their native populations difficult for some industrial countries. Consequently, millions of guest workers have been sent home. While this exodus has ameliorated the unemployment problem in northwestern Europe, it has only worsened that in the home countries of the guest workers. If these returning workers cannot find work in their home countries, and it does not seem likely that they can, their dissatisfaction could well be politically destabilizing.

As the 70's pass, it is becoming clear that expanding unemployment constitutes one of the world's gravest social ills. As unemployment levels climb, the distribution of income within a society invariably worsens and further aggravates social inequities and political stresses. It is an issue that is certain to occupy political leaders, as well as the unemployed themselves, for some time to come.

8
Security and Human Needs

The military threat to national security is only one of many that governments must now address. The numerous new threats derive directly or indirectly from the rapidly changing relationship between humanity and the earth's natural systems and resources. The unfolding stresses in this relationship initially manifest themselves as ecological stresses and resource scarcities. Later they translate into economic stresses—inflation, unemployment, capital scarcity and monetary instability. Ultimately, these economic stresses convert into social unrest and political instability.

National defense establishments are useless against these new threats. Neither bloated military budgets nor highly sophisticated weapons systems can halt the deforestation or solve the firewood crisis now affecting so many third world countries. Blocking external aggression may be a relatively simple matter compared with arresting the deterioration of local ecological systems.

Needed: a Shift in Priorities

The new threats to national security are extraordinarily complex. Ecologists understand that the deteriorating relationship between 4 billion humans and the earth's biological systems cannot continue. But political leaders have yet to grasp the social significance of this unsustainable situation.

Analyzing and understanding the nature and scale of these new threats to national security will challenge the information-gathering and analytical skills of governments. Unfortunately, the decision-making apparatus in most governments is not organized to balance threats of a traditional military nature with those of ecological and economic origins. Many political leaders perceive the new threats to security dimly, if at all. Intelligence agencies are organized to alert political leaders to potential military threats, but there is no counterpart network for warning of a collapse of a biological system. Military strategists understand the nature of military threats. Energy analysts understand the need to shift from oil to alternative energy sources, and ecologists understand the need to arrest ecological deterioration. But few individuals are trained or able to weigh and evaluate such a diversity of threats and then to translate such an assessment into the allocation of public resources that provides the greatest national security.

If military threats are considered in isolation, military strength of adversaries or potential adversaries can be measured in terms of the number of men under arms, the number and effectiveness of tanks, planes, and other military equipment, and (where the superpowers are concerned) the number of nuclear warheads and delivery missiles. Given the desire to be somewhat stronger than one's opponents, those fashioning the military budget can argue precisely and convincingly for a heavy commitment of public resources to the manufacture of weapons.

Nonmilitary threats to a nation's security are much less clearly defined than military ones. They are often the result of cumulative processes that ultimately lead to the collapse of biological systems or to the depletion of a country's oil reserves. These processes in themselves are seldom given much thought until they pass a critical threshold and disaster strikes. Thus, it is easier in the government councils of developing countries to justify expenditures for the latest-model jet fighters than for family planning to arrest the population growth that leads to food scarcity. Likewise, in industrial societies vast expenditures on long-range missiles are easier to obtain than the investments in energy conservation needed to buy time to develop alternative energy sources.

The purpose of national security deliberations should not be to maximize military strength but to maximize national security. If this latter approach were used, public resources would be distributed more widely among the many threats to national security—both the traditional military one and the newer, less precisely measured ones.

The purpose of this paper is not to argue for specific military budget cuts. Rather it is to suggest that profound new threats to the security of nations are arising and that these need to be fully considered along with the traditional ones. Only then can national security be optimized. The time for discarding long-standing and outmoded assumptions held by the governments of the superpowers is long overdue. The U.S.-Soviet relationship has changed markedly over the years, becoming less belligerent and more cooperative than it once was. During the current decade the Soviets have come to rely heavily on the United States for food, and Western banks and corporations have developed enough confidence in Soviet integrity to extend to the Soviet Union several billion dollars worth of loans and credits. But military expenditures in the two countries do not reflect this new relationship.

Lags in reordering budgetary allocations to confront the new threats to national security are glaring. In the year 1977, global expenditures on arms research are six times those for energy research, but all nations might be far more secure if this ratio were reversed. Even though a 3 percent annual population growth rate in a third world country (which translates into a 19-fold increase in a century) can destroy a country's ecological system and social structure more effectively than a foreign adversary ever could, expenditures on population education and family planning are often negligible or nonexistent. Countries will expend large sums on tanks and planes to defend their territorial sovereignty but nothing to conserve the soil on which their livelihoods depend.

A scarcity of vital resources such as oil or grain could lead to intense competition among countries for supplies, a competition that could easily escalate into military conflict. Competition between Iceland and Britain over the North Atlantic cod fisheries, between India and Bangladesh over the waters of the Ganges, and between Mexican and U.S. workers for jobs in the United States all manifest the new threats to national economic security posed by scarcity.

The continuing focus of governments on military threats to security may not only exclude attention to the newer threats, but may also make the effective address of the latter more difficult. The heavy military emphasis on national security can absorb budgetary resources, management skills and scientific talent that should be devoted to the new nonmilitary threats. Given the enormous investment required to shift the global economy from oil to alternative energy sources, one might well ask whether the world could afford the sustained large-scale use of military might of the sort deployed in World Wars I and II. Indeed, the absurdity of the traditional view is pointed out by science-fiction writer Isaac Asimov: "Even a nonnuclear war cannot be fought because it is too energy-rich a phenomenon." We cannot afford such extravagance, contends Asimov, "and are going to have to use all our energy to stay alive" with none "to spare for warfare." In effect, there simply may not be enough fuel to operate both tanks and tractors. At some point governments will be forced either to realign priorities in a manner responsive to the new threats or to watch their national security deteriorate.

The scientific talent required to make the energy transition and to prevent the destruction of biological systems is enormous. The all-out mobilization that circumstances call for entails, among other things, shifting part of that one-fourth of the world's scientific talent now employed in the military sector to the energy sector. At a time when oil reserves are being depleted, developing new energy systems may be more essential to a nation's survival than new weapons systems.

Apart from the heavy claim on public resources, the continuing exorbitant investment in armaments contributes to a psychological climate of suspicion and mistrust that makes the cooperative international address of new threats to the security of nations next to impossible. Conversely, a reduction in military expenditures by major powers would likely lead to a more cooperative attitude among national governments.

National vs. Global Security

In a world that is not only ecologically interdependent but economically and politically interdependent as well, the concept of "national" security is no longer adequate. Individual countries must respond to global crises because national governments are still the principal decision-makers, but many threats to security require a coordinated international response. The times call for efforts to secure the global systems on which nations depend. If the global climatic system is inadvertently altered by human activity, all countries will be affected. If the international monetary system is not secure, all national economies will suffer. If countries do not cooperate and preserve oceanic fisheries, food prices everywhere will rise. But political leaders have yet to realize that national security is meaningless without global security.

In some situations, countries could be drawn together into a variety of cooperative efforts to cope with shared problems. The Soviet need for assured access to U.S. grain, for example, has led to a five-year U.S.-Soviet grain agreement, and to strengthened economic ties between the two superpowers. Similarly, Middle Eastern oil-exporting countries have turned to Western banks for assistance in the management of their vast financial reserves.

In the late 20th century the key to national security is sustainability. If the biological underpinnings of the global economic system cannot be secured, then the long-term economic outlook is grim indeed. If new energy sources and systems are not in place as the oil wells begin to go dry, then severe economic disruptions are inevitable.

Perhaps the best contemporary definition of national security is one by Franklin P. Huddle, director of the U.S. congressional study, *Science, Technology and American Diplomacy*. In *Science*, Huddle writes that "National security requires a stable economy

United Nations

**The UN General Assembly, where 149 nations
discuss world problems**

with assured supplies of materials for industry. In this sense, frugality and conservation of materials are essential to our national security. Security means more than safety from hostile attack; it includes the preservation of a system of civilization."

A forceful argument can now be made that considerations of security are meaningful only when the global threats to security are taken into account. Neither individual security nor national security can be sensibly considered in isolation. In effect, the traditional military concept of "national security" is growing ever less adequate as nonmilitary threats grow more formidable.

Talking It Over

A Note for Students and Discussion Groups

This pamphlet, like its predecessors in the HEADLINE Series, is published for every serious reader, specialized or not, who takes an interest in the subject. Many of our readers will be in classrooms, seminars or community discussion groups. Particularly with them in mind, we present below some discussion questions—suggested as a starting point only—and references for further reading.

Discussion Questions

Historically, how did it happen that the idea of "national security" came to be viewed, in the United States and elsewhere, primarily in military terms? Do you agree or disagree with the author's view that this definition is not adequate in today's world? Why?

In his concluding chapter the author says "a coordinated international response" is needed to deal with threats to the nations' security from such causes as climate change, monetary disorder, depletion of fisheries and other food sources, etc. What international efforts are you aware of in these fields? How would you propose to make them more effective?

Many authorities expect the world to begin running short of oil—that is, for world oil consumption to begin to exceed new oil discoveries—sometime in the 1980's. When this happens, what alternative energy sources will be available? Do you think they will be ready to replace oil? If not, and energy consumption has to be curtailed, how would you propose to maintain employment and rising living standards for those in need?

One result of unprecedentedly rapid population growth, especially in less-developed countries, is a rise in the number of job-seekers who migrate to more-affluent countries, often illegally. What does this trend imply for the security of nations? How would you deal with it?

The author discusses the effect on biological systems, such as forests and farmlands, when man's use of them continually exceeds their "carrying capacity." What economic and human problems will this trend create if long continued? What solutions do you think are likely to work best (a) in the United States, (b) in developing countries?

Are you aware of recent international efforts to forestall new outbreaks of malnutrition and starvation in such regions as South Asia and the African Sahel? In your opinion, how effective are these efforts, and what could be done to make them more so?

It has been pointed out that the national budgets of the United States and other countries show a larger expenditure on military forces than, for example, on education or health services. Do you think it is possible for nations to agree to redirect some of their efforts from military to constructive social programs? How would you propose to bring about such a change?

READING REFERENCES

1. Energy

Eckholm, Erik, "The Other Energy Crisis: Firewood." Worldwatch Paper 1. Washington, D.C., Worldwatch Institute, September 1975.

Hayes, Denis, *Rays of Hope: The Transition to a Post-Petroleum World.* New York, Norton, 1977. (Paperback.)

———, "Nuclear Power: The Fifth Horseman." Worldwatch Paper 6. Washington, D.C., Worldwatch Institute, May 1976.

The National Research Council, *Energy and Climate: Studies in Geophysics.* Washington, D.C., National Academy of Science, 1977.

2. Food and Ecology

Brown, Lester R., "Our Daily Bread." HEADLINE Series 225. New York, Foreign Policy Association, April 1975.

———, "The Politics and Responsibility of the North American Breadbasket." Worldwatch Paper 2. Washington, D.C., Worldwatch Institute, October 1975.

Eckholm, Erik P., *Losing Ground: Environment Stress and World Food Prospects.* New York, Norton, 1976. (Paperback.)

Eckholm, Erik and Brown, Lester R., "Spreading Deserts—The Hand of Man." Worldwatch Paper 13. Washington, D.C., Worldwatch Institute, August 1977.

Shepherd, Jack, *The Politics of Starvation.* Washington, D.C., Carnegie Endowment for International Peace, 1975.

3. Population and Health

Brown, Lester R., McGrath, Patricia L. and Stokes, Bruce, "Twenty-two Dimensions of the Population Problem." Worldwatch Paper 5. Washington D.C., Worldwatch Institute, March 1976.

Brown, Lester R., "World Population Trends: Signs of Hope, Signs of Stress." Worldwatch Paper 8. Washington D.C., Worldwatch Institute, October 1976.

Eckholm, Erik P., *The Picture of Health: Environmental Sources of Disease.* New York, Norton, 1977. (Paperback.)

Stokes, Bruce, "Filling the Family Planning Gap." Worldwatch Paper 12. Washington, D.C., Worldwatch Institute, May 1977.

4. General, Social and Political

Brown, Lester R., *The Twenty-Ninth Day.* New York, Norton. Publication date: March 1978. (Paperback.)

———, *In the Human Interest.* New York, Norton, 1974. (Paperback.)

Sivard, Ruth Leger, *World Military and Social Expenditures 1977.* Leesburg, Va., WMSE Publications, 1977.

Statement of Ownership, Management and Circulation

(Required by 39 U.S.C. 3685)

1. Title of publication: HEADLINE SERIES. 1a. Publication No: 238340.
2. Date of filing: September 29, 1977.
3. Frequency of issue: 5 times each year—Feb., Apr., June, Oct., Dec.
3a. No. of issues published annually: 5.
3b. Annual subscription price: $7.00.
4. Location of known office of publication: 345 E. 46th St., New York, N.Y. 10017.
5. Location of the headquarters or general business offices of the publishers: Same.

6. Names and complete addresses of publisher, editor, and managing editor: Publisher—Foreign Policy Association, 345 E. 46th St., New York, N.Y. 10017; Editor—Wallace Irwin, Jr., 345 E. 46th St., New York, N.Y. 10017; Managing Editor—None.

7. Owner: (If owned by a corporation, its name and address must be stated and also immediately thereunder the names and addresses of stockholders owning or holding 1 percent or more of total amount of stock. If not owned by a corporation, the names and addresses of the individual owners must be given. If owned by a partnership or other unincorporated firm, its name and address, as well as that of each individual must be given.) Foreign Policy Association, Inc., 345 E. 46th St., New York, N.Y. 10017.

8. Known bondholders, mortgagees, and other security holders owning or holding 1 percent or more of total amount of bonds, mortgages or other securities: (If there are none, so state) none.

9. For Completion by Nonprofit Organizations Authorized to Mail at Special Rates (Section 132.122, PSM): The purpose, function, and nonprofit status of this organization and the exempt status for Federal income tax purposes have not changed during preceding 12 months.

10.	Extent and Nature of Circulation	Average No. Copies Each Issue During Preceding 12 Months	Actual Number of Copies of Single Issue Published Nearest to Filing Date
A.	Total no. copies printed (Net Press Run)	16,066 incl. reprints	15,176
B.	Paid Circulation 1. Sales through dealers and carriers, street vendors and counter sales	4,006	538
	2. Mail subscriptions.	6,996	6,811
C.	Total paid circulation	11,002	7,349
D.	Free distribution by mail, carrier or other means Samples, complimentary, and other free copies	1,014	247
E.	Total distribution (Sum of C and D)	12,016	7,596
F.	Copies not distributed 1. Office use, left over, unaccounted, spoiled after printing 2. Returns from news agents	4,050 none	7,580 none
G.	Total (Sum of E, F1 and 2—should equal net press run shown in A)	16,066	15,176

I certify that the statements made by me above are correct and complete.

DON DENNIS,
Business Manager